BETWEEN THE YEARS

LYNN COHEN

BLUE LIGHT PRESS ✦ 1ST WORLD PUBLISHING

1ST WORLD
PUBLISHING

SAN FRANCISCO ✦ FAIRFIELD ✦ DELHI

1ST WORLD LIBRARY
PO Box 2211
Fairfield, IA 52556
www.1stworldpublishing.com

BLUE LIGHT PRESS
www.bluelightpress.com
Email: bluelightpress@aol.com

BOOK & COVER DESIGN
Melanie Gendron
melaniegendron999@gmail.com

COVER PHOTO
Aaron Donahue, taken by his mother, Carrie Cohen, daughter of Lynn Cohen

FIRST EDITION

Library of Congress Control Number: 2017958912

ISBN 9781421837963

This book is dedicated to my grandson,
Aaron Jacob Donahue,
the smartest person I know.

In Memoriam
Peggy Lemle (1921 – 2016), my aunt,
who always loved my poetry.

ACKNOWLEDGMENTS

I would like to acknowledge the poignantly talented poets that have inspired me: W. S. Merwin, Phillip Lopate, T. S. Eliot, William Butler Yeats, Robert Pinsky, Frank Bidart, Ron Padgett, Barbara Novak, Galway Kinnel, Natasha Trethewey, Sarah Teasdale, D. H. Lawrence, and the rest.

I would also particularly like to thank the poet Edmund Miller, Senior Professor in the English Department at LIU–Post, for his support and careful editorial eye.

TABLE OF CONTENTS

I.   Between the Years

     1.   Cornelia Street Café
     2.   Cornelia Street Café Revisited
     3.   The Year the Bay Froze
     4.   "We Are between the Years."
     5.   Vivid Images
     6.   St. Mark's
     7.   Lone Star Days
     9.   Ninth Birthday
     10.   Dream Life
     11.   City of Glass
     12.   Oak Beach Inn after Sandy
     13.   Dare to Dream
     14.   At the Laundromat
     15.   "Huis Clos"
     16.   North Square Hotel

II.   Time Passes

     19.   La Naissance
     20.   Summer 2011
     21.   May Crowning
     22.   Rouge Moonlight
     23.   "How far away the stars …"
     24.   "Walking on stilts through time"
     25.   "Quantum Continuum"
     26.   May 1968
     28.   Blueberry Memories
     29.   Dover
     30.   Irish Callings
     31.   The Shadows and Beyond
     32.   Saisons
     33.   Affairs Are Not for the Faint Hearted
     34.   Summer at the Post Office
     35.   Time Does Not Pass

III.   People Revisited

    39.   Cha-Cha-Cha
    40.   Gretchen
    41.   For My Mother on the Death of Nixon
    42.   May Again
    43.   I Become Twenty-Three
    44.   Drifting
    45.   Child of a Boy
    46.   The First Woman You Made Love To
    47.   South Pacific Legends
    48.   Metamorphosis

IV.   Le Temps retrouvé

    51.   Confession
    52.   Holy Communion
    53.   Dispensation
    54.   Genuflection
    55.   Hirsute
    56.   The Garden
    57.   Words on the Page
    58.   The Language of Spring
    59.   Feeling Cold
    60.   Lunching
    61.   Don't Stop Time
    62.   "Armageddon in the Afternoon"
    63.   Dark Fog
    64.   Moments in Time
    65.   Colossus
    66.   Imaginings
    67.   "The Library of Babel"
    68.   Ancient Images
    69.   Endings

    71.   About the Author
    73.   Publications, Lectures, Grants

I. BETWEEN THE YEARS

CORNELIA STREET CAFÉ

Another summer
at the Cornelia Street Café
where we sipped wine
layered time
between the hors d'œurves
and sidewalk art shows
with wide-eyed girl paintings
and passing pedigreed pups.

Inside the poet read
seated and trembling
scotch on one side
a *New Yorker* magazine nearby.

You switched seats
and became so close
I could taste your poetry
brush your knee and
feel your hand climbing mine.

I know this was real
because we were friends
then enemies and
now I barely recognize your
jowls and deep lines,
the bald spots and stooped posture
that are the present.

CORNELIA STREET CAFÉ REVISITED

Through my decades
white wicker chairs
fronted the Cornelia Street Café
like those at Paris eateries
on the Champs Élysées
far from Père Lachaise.

Where the years reappear
as a circle of sad memories—
different men differentiating the days.
And dying . . . .
And dying.

Could we have stood
near the Café
before we ever met
gazing through the other?
You commuting to NYU from Brooklyn
I married, unhappy, lost—
a situation you would deny inheriting
despite your constant dabbling

THAT YEAR THE BAY FROZE

They carried you over snow drifts.
They so tall.
You so small—
at five.

That year the bay froze
we skated over a brine world
past ice fishermen
trolling for their winter catch
before and after global warming.

You live in my memories
of a shared egg salad sandwich
cut in squares with onions
cut fingers rubbed together
before HIV fears
blood sisters.

Later on, they lied about your divorce.
You had never been married
only engaged.
How could the following forty years disappear?
I can find them in my mind,
share each instant
within my tortured being
this overtly cold season
as the bay is freezing again,
and my tears stream down
in tiny rivulets
for what has been lost
and what has been found.
Perhaps, they are the same.

"WE ARE BETWEEN THE YEARS."

—Samuel Beckett to Desmond Egan in a Paris Café

Winter unfolds in images:
leggings and childhood igloos
dogs pulling sleds
through neighborhoods
I dare revisit only in memory
as I travel through parallel pasts—
hers and mine—
the years intertwine
like time
in a Faulkner novel.

The canines look the same,
and if I look farther,
she is in a house dress,
draped in laziness,
feasting on salami on matzo smeared with butter,
and a filter-less Camel chaser.
Then Dewars— "No water please."
She read away her days.
Hattie cleaned.
Mrs. Sherry typed.
Dark Shadows played forbiddingly in the background.
Childhood I have long repressed.
Days after months after years it was—
it must have been.

VIVID IMAGES

In vivid images
you invade my sleep
traipsing a street
where the year is unclear:
your wife wears deep pink,
pushes an empty stroller.

Prêt à porter
in Burberry you twirl
a tiny girl
chuckling and flashing your caps
near the Bryant Park carousel,
ice skaters,
winter crêperies,
bouquinistes and
upper-class eateries in
tents heated by kerosene
transparent like the Winter Palace.

ST. MARK'S

The ghost of Ginsberg
floats
above the poems
remnants of his skull remain
on the stage
not the late-in-life poet
in his Gap Ad splendor
early Ginsberg
in combat boots
army fatigues
Dad camouflaged at his side
nearby
young police loiter
Kent-state style
inside teach-ins begin:
"How not to get arrested"
Today's Ginsbergs
in dreds, drag, sheer skirts
applaud anarchy
raise their fists revolutionary style
shake from their meds
make mad love in the summer heat,
and I wonder,
"What year is this"?
This faux revolt:
Columbia 1967?
Syracuse 1970?
No, I conclude:
it is just a time people go on brief pilgrimages
modern-day Chaucerian characters
journeying away from convention
players in the living theater of their souls

LONE STAR DAYS

I remember
my grandmother's forbidden jellies
grape and strawberry
crushed beneath paraffin
in neat rows of glass jars
as I paraded before her
all black and pink and thin
to get a brief arabesque of praise

I swirled in lightheaded starvation
twirled in a doily-lined living room
Weehawken, New Jersey
circa 1958
a meeting of the club blue eyes
Stuart studying
Frank in Hoboken
And forever seventeen
on that not yet stereo

But this is only in my mind's eye
for when I close the curtain
all I see are
your eyes steel
in their blue-gray coldness
paralleling your mocking white beard

I wish I could tear through *The Years*
blond and thin, short and
tousled and colt-like
She controlled my present
Though we never met
She scarred my life

In her Lone Star Days
She stole your wet tongue-thrust kisses
Even when she did not want them
So it's over
And it never was.

NINTH BIRTHDAY

So many years ago when
I was nine
my mother made fried chicken
and angel food cake
gave me an indoor pool party

Years before summer camp
and the Cuban Missile Crisis
and Bay of Pigs invasion
predating my first boyfriends
with their sloppy smacks
on my inexperienced lips
running their hands up my back
Christmas, Miami Beach 1963

Decades before college
the women's movement and civil rights
peace protests
where everyone was slaughtered
ages before marriage
and a child

DREAM LIFE

There are things I pretend not to notice
green, tiny sparkles
on dull, white walls
rain that beats
like locusts
in my dream life
one-hundred years post-Freud
I am a failed analysand
no H. D.* me

As I watch us fold
in motionless time
remake of Marienbad
I wander through your gardens
as you hold my mind

My damp, yellow hair
tangled over your hazel eyes
falls in humid clumps
on a January night
that feels like May

*Hilda Doolittle is a poet who was analyzed by Freud.

CITY OF GLASS

So many years ago
when transparency meant clear glass,
and green was the color of grass
my family rode
in an ancient station wagon
to the City of Glass
to acquire seedlings for
a summer harvest
our black clone canines barking in the back
my sister and I quarreling constantly
foreshadowing a life-long battle
Then, I believed in spring
that rebirth would always be
even though I had not read Hemingway
nor been to France.

OAK BEACH INN AFTER SANDY

"Home is where one starts from."
—T. S. Eliot, "East Coker" section of *The Four Quartets*

The broken platform juts
just barely over the Bay
inside
past moments replay
at the bare bar
and on empty ebony floors

Outside
your eager lips
still exist
and resonate
with smacking waves
on eroded beaches
hidden by tall weeds
on a fall midnight

In the longed-for East
Lindenhurst and Lawrence
you lie with what was
coffee thermos in hand
a solipsistic moment
of hybrid haze

DARE TO DREAM

I dare to dream when
your hair hangs in damp clumps
through a May mist and
mine billows between the rings
he blew in a past century:
blue-white smoke
floating.

My vision of his visage
tanned and scratchy
masks your rhythms–
cadences blanketed to mine.

And I dare to dream
of another spring,
when greenery
shades summer's roads
and I mourn humid mornings
that will never come again
crying for all who will not see another fall and
wondering
just wondering.

AT THE LAUNDROMAT

Front teeth missing
she folds my sheets
daydreams of a man "thirty or so"
who lives near Nicolls Road
and is wrong for her,
her friend says—
As they giggle,
she blushes—
and they smoke and smoke
scratch endless lottery tickets,
believe in dreams.

I marvel at how different we are.
My dentist reattaches my caps.
I do not do laundry—
do not like younger men,
and I am more complex,
of course.

Or maybe just a better liar.
All my men are wrong.
I planned a marriage in Jersey, if you won the lottery.
I am no fool.
Mutual property states all the way.
Yet we have never gone all the way.
Barely touched
Merely brushed lips
Too tenderly

"HUIS CLOS"

—Jean-Paul Sartre

No escape—
from haunting dreams:
where my parents linger in darkness
rising above stone markers and
reliving ordinary days:
showers, smokes, ironing, cereal.

Childhood I left in another century
a different world
where camp and girl scouts
clamming and cleaning fluke
were not foreshadows of assassinations nor
twentieth-first century terrorism;
we feared the cold war
and atom bomb
not the suicide bomber and Islamic extremists

NORTH SQUARE HOTEL

At the North Square Hotel,
where MacDougal meets Waverly,
just past the Arch at Fifth and the Park,
I move back into my past as
elegant edifices still front the square, and I
pass my grandmother's apartment and NYU.

We stayed at her apartment
high above Washington Square
walked hand-in-hand to Barnes & Noble
loved on endless evenings
kisses and clothes long out of the way
bathing in the sweat of city summer nights.

The Fantastics playing permanently in the Village
fountains spraying
musicians playing through the seventies

I miss the casual sex and
one-night stands
when they were safe.
Today I settle for love, affection and attention.

II. TIME PASSES

LA NAISSANCE

for Aaron

I remember the cord wrapped your neck
as you gasped for breath
in your gray naissance;
the misdiagnosis
from that foreign doctor
that hot summer night
at that dark city hospital,
where I easily parked in front.

Now, your avocado-shaped eyes,
cheeks the color of fall squash,
hair tinted by blackberries
hint at when
I will not be here to see
the man you become.

Meanwhile, lost in primal language,
lungs belying tour premature birth,
you scream through the days.
Frustration impossible to face
as rubber ducks swim out of reach,
and cereal jars are emptied.

SUMMER 2011

Up the whole night
street lights streaming the blinds
yellow flashes of taxis and trucks a constant
crisis ridden 24-hours become another:
more laundry
more diapers
more screams.

The pediatrician reminds you you are a new parent;
you feel like a vache:
white milk replacing the Red Door
the breast pump breaking is
a bigger calamity than the country shutting down

Baby has his own closet
so many clothes he will not wear
size newborn not appropriate for his Bar Mitzvah

Flip-flops have become the new Jimmy Choo shoes,
a pair of Manolo Blahniks is only viewed on *Sex and the City*,
and your television is permanently turned to *Sesame Street*

MAY CROWNING

for Julien Strong

You walk away from baby days
diaper dragging
giggling and proud.

Last year, you were not even here.
Now, you are precious in plaid.
Sweet like mint flowers in childhood's golden verses
while lush purple peonies
lace the lawn and
early morning light strobes
a tiger swallowtail's flight.

On this May maple sugar-making morning
before you move from babyhood,
sleep one more night tight in moonlight.

ROUGE MOONLIGHT

Syria 2013:
bombing shatters rouge moonlight,
mirrors monsoons, where
no clouds appear.

At home, my fingers find
a channel without war
Sesame Street from 1984
provides relief when
Big Bird squawks the ABCs.

Still my mind wanders,
and I wonder, if the president is honest.
Three wars are three more than he promised.
Fear my last lover is a CIA agent—
I was always suspicious
that a Bensonhurst boy,
who speaks Russian and Arabic
spends his days teaching elementary grades
always wondered why he was so repressed
he could barely graze my lips
stared rather than touched
pulled me tighter than tight . . . then let go.
Could it be because I said "no"?
because I was confused, too

"HOW FAR AWAY THE STARS . . ."

"How far away the stars seem, and how far
Is our first kiss, and ah, how old my heart."
—William Butler Yeats

My muse—
fingers my blonde curls,
lip syncs to the music
moves with the beat
of his recent teens
kisses me too hard for
someone his mom's age,
while I feel foam on his face.

We see the same stars,
wander the Salley Gardens,
cuddle at Coole,
dream of County Sligo and
grass that is always green.

My muse—
has never been to Paris,
never strolled the Bois de Boulogne
among cherry blossoms;
his life's alive with possibilities,
while mine has responsibilities.
He is my poker hand,
the game I cannot play again.

"WALKING ON STILTS THROUGH TIME"

—Marcel Proust

Quiet Irish evenings when
streets stretch to the Liffey and
back to pubs and private poker clubs
orange stripes slice the turquoise sky–
night sunlight abides as
"I am walking on stilts through time":
And journeying back to Joyce's Dublin
street map in tow.

"QUANTUM CONTINUUM"

—Barbara Novak

Time bends like a quantum continuum:
Billy Pilgrim's travels to Tralfamadore
Borges's encounters with enemies, friends, strangers—
all "autonomous moments"
jardins des roses
that multifoliate flower
of memory
The eternal present can never be omnipresent
only a search for redemption.

MAY 1968

I remember still
spring hung like moss at Tara.
And we clung to time
as though there would be no more.
In the eroding ocean beaches,
we explored the hard, sandy slopes,
watched the wet reeds overhead,
heard the thrusting of the tides.

Thirty-five years have passed.
My wedding album more a cemetery directory.
Between battlefield briefs,
the news barks "Fire Island is disappearing;
Field five gone
already."

Still I remember March 2003:
We strolled
Timeless
Ecstatic
Coffee cups
Cigarette butts
Forbidden love
Hester Prynne in tandem
Mirror images
Dostoevskian doubles
Not idiots.

My moods self-immolate
Still
Incarcerate.
Incense me
I cannot deal with frustration
Have no patience
Yesterday is my bible.

BLUEBERRY MEMORIES

Your poetry full with summer berries—
succulent and never enough—
flashes back like forties' film noir,
is surreal like Buñuel,*
floats through the formal gardens at Marienbad
screaming "l'année prochaine,"
encapsulates a search for lost time:
Georgia 1980s,
Napa in the nineties,
a woman twice dismissed,
wine and Waldbaums,
the places we have all been.

*Spanish film maker of *Un Chien andalou (Andalusian Dog)*, a 1929
surrealist film.

DOVER

A goddess mounts
hard cliffs:
bare through Kent, Canterbury, Cardiff
her hair floats through the years
eyes olive green
the fruit of Tuscan trees
slanted like Asian oranges
in the lost markets
of her unconscious
on a ripe summer morning
the cornucopia of life

Be her host
let her ride you
through undersea tunnels
share orgiastic promises
procreative and primal
primitive reed-covered thrusts
sharp and unforgiving
as purgatorial pirates
sail past orbs

All the flowers are evil
in the rose-gardens
of memory
sanctified symbols
and sacred ladies
dance to your cadence
prostrate at the feet of your poems'
strophes and meters

IRISH CALLINGS

Tree branch cutouts
cover a July sky
thick humidity hangs
over the Bog of Allen.

Remembering shared pints
and camaraderie in Dublin pubs,
the eerie whispering of the dead
reverberating on earth
as they call the living to join them.

In the cool mornings
and sun-filled nights
of the Emerald Isle,
I read the daily racing sheets
enjoy Irish tea and breakfast.

All I have to worry about are
is the country going out of business in my absence and
has Ireland collapsed before my arrival—
in addition to a grandchild, who did not exist during my last trip.

THE SHADOWS AND BEYOND

Could it be only tea
your invitation to me?
Faces facing opposite walls
obscured by steam
from hot, strong scents
always English Breakfast
always plain scones without jam
warm, wrapped in clothe
grasped by long, tapered fingers
so late in life
a birthday in common.
We were born under Taurus
right down to long marriages
despite your hidden wife
wine-laden life
twenty-first century strife
the poems pour on
in the shadows and beyond.

SAISONS

Cherry blossoms bloom
back lit by pink skies
where your poems swirl in time,
and our bodies entwine:
lips suckling
in hidden shadows
among spring birthing
and summer slaughter
we reap a season of lust
as puddles form a pool, and
sweaters fall to the floor
awaiting the mating,
the mélange of mixed-up souls
on forbidden afternoons when
entanglements ribbon together
in serpentine splendor—
ebb and flow nowhere

AFFAIRS ARE NOT FOR THE FAINT HEARTED

VFW tri-corner covering his brow
afternoon cheek scrub
gracing his face
bagel and Joe in hand
he comes to see her—
calls her his "lady."
The senior center's chess game and tray lunches
can wait to another day.

Despite wrinkled cheeks
silver wig and
gnarled wrists
she is his Jezebel between the sheets.

Two late-in-life lovers
their spouses long gone,
or so I suppose
until the talk turns to his wife at home
her husband in a nursing home,
and I know affairs are not for the faint hearted.

SUMMER AT THE POST OFFICE

Will we look like that:
hats covering missing hair and
all the years
worn raincoats
worn on summer days
so long out of style
I cannot remember them ever
being in style
in seven decades?

And I wonder what they see.
Perhaps, her turquoise flowered scarf
and his tan derby
doing a duet and
climbing into an SUV.

TIME DOES NOT PASS

White marble:
Four-dimensional
Holographic
Seen from everywhere
The World's Fair
The Pietà

Languid and gum popping
Catholic school skirt hitched high
She kissed you on line
Your first time

I scored the year before
A Miami Beach cabana
We wondered why we felt nothing
He knew about running his fingers up my back
But not how

That would wait for another summer
The slim lust of early teens
Damp rec halls
Swapping tongues
Sharing teeth

Over forty years have passed
Yet when you hold me
Stroke me
Kiss me
I know
Time does not pass

III. PEOPLE REVISITED

CHA-CHA-CHA

for Aunt Rose

Wearing shoes with Cuban heels
soles making rat-tap sounds
Aunt Rose taught the Cha-Cha-Cha
through many Catskill Mountain summers.

She worked in the Lodge's
damp recreation hall
and private cottages
on dark evenings.

And when she was hit by a bus,
the Lodge had long been closed, and
Rose by then an octogenarian, who
had lied about her age for decades,
became wheelchair bound and mute
wore adult diapers—
communicated through gestures and grabbing.

My mother was sick,
so I took over:
brought Rose the dog for pet therapy
arranged for a beautician
bought her a television.

And when she was gone,
on soft summer nights
mixing with distant fog horns
the sounds of her "Cha-Cha-Cha"
could still be heard reverberating.

GRETCHEN

She is always there:
statuesque and bare
near Lake Michigan
where the winds whip your past
present
her presence is close to my pen
hair hanging
eyes glazed

So I leave for Long Island
Where his mirror reflects bound-feet memories
The Orient
A half century past
Women whispering submissively
in Ho Chi Minh City
obis and buns pushed back

And I play dominoes with my nephew
while you dream of Paris.
I know it never worked for me.
When I was twenty,
I wandered the Seine alone
thought of joining lovers at the Louvre
even entering a painting would do
especially Manet's Le Déjeuner sur l'herbe
with its nude
Le Pyramide went the way of the rose.
I am not sure I ever had a rose-garden.
The men I chose were taken:
By addictions
By wives
By other men
By their own lives
Does it really make a difference?

FOR MY MOTHER ON THE DEATH OF NIXON

The calendar has its own agenda
splattering grayness
like brisk raindrops
against my late spring face
flipping through events
that are as irrevocable
as any in a history text

For my history
is a pattern
a lineage
of photographs
staring above my desk
resemblances of other times
other people
some gone now
all eventually
black/white, colors, years

The late morning sun
does not reflect my mood
forty-four moons later
in this fifth decade
I mourn for Nixon
in my mother's stead

MAY AGAIN

for Ira and Spike and Laura

Like a Syracuse rain
drops splatter at the train window
and drift my mind
out past trees
too bare for May
where for just that year
sweet-aired spring
danced in on timetable
in the places
where we loved:
worn cars
drive-in movies
lakes
all promising of summer
in that 1968 world
that I never doubted
would stretch ahead for years

I BECOME TWENTY-THREE

Rainy day scenes
still lives fading
into unfocused dreams
walking past Paley Park
this late April day
caught among longings
for youth's past
dances and hand holding
yesterdays
and wistful glimpses
past yet unopened
window worlds

DRIFTING

for Johnny

I am running out of decades
away from the moment
that is a fleece casket
in a winter burial

In your world
it is always summer:
cows perpetually give birth,
chickens lay eggs
and the slaughterhouses are
six hours away

I will drift with you
on the tip of your mind—
lose hours as though they were never mine
lose consciousness of all time

I will float
through your fantasies
mindless and find
my hands raking your chest
tied to a past
I can't untie from
But am lifted
in supernatural ways

To days
that will not go away so
unwrap your presents
one after the other,
And I will drift.

CHILD OF A BOY

for Tom Law

My child of a boy,
don't long, cold nights
haunt you
now that you have known
those hazy, dimly-lit
days after days,
those tender, timeless times
when shadows and light
lost their meaning?

My child of a boy
can you return
to a lost world
as if
it had always been?
Can you forget centuries
as if
they never were?

THE FIRST WOMAN YOU MADE LOVE TO

for Brian Arkins, NUI Galway

Sheep dot the green, gentle slopes;
goats give milk for cheese;
you are young and professorial,
classic and courtly
among Joycean wild flowers
in the damp meadows–
daisies and wisteria blowing softly
entwined with the first woman you made love to,
who strayed in a few days,
causing you to raise glasses of Guinness
in Galway pubs
sashay your hips
strut your stuff
while reading Gaelic poems and singing Irish ballads
your dark hair turning white and then gray
before leaving forever
as summers passed one into another.

SOUTH PACIFIC LEGENDS

South Pacific legends
from my father's tales—
belie the bloody battles
he never mentions outside his journals.

His mango and coconut memories
of exotic women draped in iridescent weaves
dancing in Officers' Clubs,
while the Canine Corps
scoured the arid land
far from Weehawken,
where my grandmother knit woolen underwear gifts
for him to wear
in a valley in Bali
in a war-torn world
as gentle beach waves blessed the decades
and became my bedtime stories.

METAMORPHOSIS

Golden flies
steamy late summer
another August lost
autumn approaches
your 57th

You wear
canvas sneakers
cracked and weary
gray as your hair
lined like your visage
matted and old
you scrunch in primal
moments
ancestral habits
entrenched

Do not drag me
by my locks
or club me
to your cave

I live in my moments
not your fantasies
it is no longer June
autumn approaches

IV. LE TEMPS RETROUVÉ

CONFESSION

I passed St. Aidan's
where you kneel and pray
blessed by St. Margaret Mary Alacoque
holy days of obligation, every Sunday
and remembered:
illicit touches
endless hugs we denied
kisses soft on softer lips
naughty missives.

We were teasing teens—
though we are not 16 . . .
players in an endless end game;
we did not say what we meant
nor mean what we said;
we had a near affair but missed it.

You have been this path before—
running partners
train companions
vixens with vibrant locks
compose your history
of daily dalliances
despite your perfect life
and literary wife.

HOLY COMMUNION

Go to God's garden;
walk among the iconography;
watch innocents form a white line;
pilgrims from Parochial school yearbooks
reborn in Chaucerian April
like pink spring blossoms.

Host reunion rooms,
where whirls of Marist girls and
west side women commune,
sip red wine, eat wafers.

See the vibrant temptress,
the teen with braids, straw hat and jeans, and
that long-ago 18-year old, who
left you in a Marine Park pub.

Go to forget the future:
Saturday evenings chasing your sister,
a dead train companion, and
the almond shaped, coal-colored eyes
of the girl with the pink umbrella,
hiding in the shadows—
of days long obliterated

DISPENSATION

Among late spring offerings,
the summer solstice nears;
my triptych concludes as
the rules relax, and
I indulge in fantasies:
crisscrossed limbs,
deep scratches on our backs,
the lunacies of the planting moon.

When fall appears
the sky streaked
by a pastiche of pumpkins and purples,
your arms will be gone from my shoulders.

And I will no longer remember
your lips tight on mine,
my resistance on walkabout.
Wondering if I invited you home,
would you say, "No,"
and I would be mortified;
would you say, "Yes,"
and I would never forgive either of us.

So I say nothing and
revel in his sport—
so like yours—
and in memories of a gas fireplace,
claw foot tub, and
the way he rubbed my soul.

GENUFLECTION

Reading Hemingway
dreaming of Montmartre
Sacré Cœur and
the Funicular
I remember
stained glass from centuries past and
the candles ready to be lighted
by the faithful genuflecting
in the shadow of St. Francis and the doves
Good Friday until Easter Sunday

Notre Dame looms on the Seine
near my bateau-mouche
both the Rive droit
and Rive gauche
call back college years:
Le Tour Eiffel
and the Musée d'Orsay
with Renoir's City and Country danseurs
young with red hats
between the years
moving effortlessly among the centuries

HIRSUTE

Would you burn in hell,
if I opened one button?
two?
traced the hair on your fingers
up your arms?
down your chest?
forgot about your comb over?
did not notice the near-bare scalp
where your hair used to be?

Wonder if you are bursting with
the greens and pinks of spring?
The perfect days finally
here again and again
as you run:
an elitist,
a near marathon man,
poet and writer
(your memoir creative nonfiction),
an actor,
trader,
chess player in an end game,
flying back and forth while
speaking Arabic and Russian.

THE GARDEN

I cannot remember a lovelier May:
soft spring days
dot distant gardens
aglow in noon light
rosebushes promise fragrant smells
scarlet tanagers build nests
lovers strut two abreast
squirrels scurry in newfound twosomes
where blood-crossed paths
host commemorative bricks
Christ in torn crimson
chiseled on cool marble slabs
new communicants lined up
to partake first wafers
communing in a sudden shower
               dampening
               shivering
               falling

WORDS ON THE PAGE

Déjà vu:
a distant Christmas celebrated
in a church in Montmartre
snow splattering stained glass
as the priest said mass

Later, when we lay fronting the fireplace of our souls
Chanukah candles flickering below
I never knew another couple so close

Forty years have passed, and
I am wary to do this again:
quiet winter hours isolated
in dreary motels,
in ice storms
while staring into the street-lamp muse
brought pain

Yet when you appear buoyant
darting like a windhover
green in fall
apple-cheeked in mid-life boyhood
naughty and adorable
I wish I had braids
for your inkwells
a straw hat, jeans and a yellow shirt
was a blonde 19-year old
who deserved everything you had

THE LANGUAGE OF SPRING

Leaves leaping to their deaths
another passing autumn
yesterday's spank-orange pumpkins
today's jack'o lanterns
kicked in the streets

Staring into the language of spring
Neither verdant nor timeless:
mud in March
misery in April
more in May

You brushed my lips
I slept
arms wrapped
around the girl I was

FEELING COLD

108—
no shade
too hot to wade
as he wraps a vest
over a pressed shirt
references his blood test
allergy to band aids
hole in his nose
feels cold
sips South African wine
speaks of his wife's loss
barren at 35
while water lilies lay like lost children
awaiting Ophelia
and the Tarot is lain
for the hanged man
swinging through years of nightmares.

LUNCHING

A lovely lunch
To any observer
Three middle-aged people
Endive, bisque, scampi

Behind the façade:
One lost a child to a speeder
and tried to join him
by overdosing on Valium
Another one's teen tried to kill herself
The final musketeer lost his roommate to a noose

All three used the right fork
among the not-so-small talk
while sipping modern-day chardonnay
in an upscale eatery

The topic was poetry
supposedly
poets who committed suicide
in ovens, in garages, in bathtubs, in rivers
poets in full makeup
as out of season as their lives

The subtopic was religion
Or lack thereof
Pantheism and animism
Close runners up
To replace monotheism
In a world of constant terrorism
A lovely lunch
In the suburbs
Three unrelated people:
An accountant, a professor, a business man

DON'T STOP TIME

I threw away the calendar
you gave me Christmas 2003:
your dog gracing every page
mine recently in the grave
each leaf engraved
with faux endearments
I lived to hear.

Yet I cannot part with the pressed roses,
the necklace that reflects my eyes, nor
the diamond-chip bracelet—
You always had such good taste.

My raconteur of boring Camille,
I adored your thoughts on *Stop Time*
and Elaine through the ages.
Even Marta,
who is smarter than I,
if she is still alive at 75.

Sadly, you have deaf ears—
so you never could hear
that I cared.
Parting gets easier when you have done it for six years.

"ARMAGEDDON IN THE AFTERNOON"

—Gladys Henderson

The seashore is a metaphor
for the corner of time and memory
luring survivors on a death march
with its Sirens' song
distant masts of long-beached ships
graves rocking in the waves.

At the corner of time and memory
everything eventually ends
at the border of sand and seascape
under dark, endless ash remains
remnants of volcanic spew,
nuclear winter or
weapons perhaps
What does it matter?

So wander the road with me
in these carnivorous days
faith has gone away
from the corner of time and memory
as other pilgrims pass
begging for food
another Holocaust perhaps.

DARK FOG

The fog lies on the mountain
heavy, dark, still
like my moods
gray seared by whiteness
clouds rolling into night
passing in chiaroscuro highs

The trees tip in the wind
and reach out
their green and birch colors
wade through endless haze

As I wonder
if in Vermont's mountains
your music reaches
miles through the stillness
if you feel
the loss and emptiness
of endless laughter
our shared times
in quiet Village cafés

The next morning
the sun hangs
on the mountain
like a lover
distant and remote
as the night before fades.

MOMENTS IN TIME

I asked you for this moment,
And you said, "No"
that I long ago committed all my time.

Yet every time I glance into the swirls
of green and blue language
that come from your eyes
everything fades
into your hair still damp
as you come to school
on an early December morning
that feels like spring
as giddily I swing my hair still golden
over the child you alone see in me.

I have nothing to give you
nearly half so nice
as the green-flecked bracelet
you gave me.

Yesterday, when I was young,
I could let moments pass
and chances fly away.
Today may be my last dance through
fields of sepia flowers,
meadows of our minds and times.

COLOSSUS

Thinking of the Colossus of Rhodes
a Wonder of the Ancient World
the Hanging Gardens of Babylon
and the Sphinx I long to visit
I wander Corfu with you
my modern-day Colossus.

Your dark Greek hair and green eyes
shine in the Mediterrancan sunlight.
We sleep along with the goats
on daytime beaches,
and I become young with the setting sun
tangled in your tanned arms
as you nuzzle my neck
and remind me how long we have waited
for these days
how many rules we did not break
to be together.

IMAGININGS

Only the imagination is real.

—William Carlos Williams

A Boy's Will is the Wind's Will.
And the Thoughts of Youth are Long, Long Thoughts.

—Henry Wadsworth Longfellow

I remember my motor boat
over fifty years ago,
where we made love among
the cadences of the quiet waves.

I lived in fantasy:
confused sex with love;
lust for forever.

And although I know
I cannot control the passing moments,
I do not mourn my gone days,
dead lovers, husband and cousins.

I can live in the present
memories-in-the-making
as my grandson turns six,
his lips open like a rosebud in spring
with the wonder of the season.

"THE LIBRARY OF BABEL"

(The title is from a short story in Jorge Luis Borges's *Ficciones*.)

Multi-colored fish swimming on your tie,
you swing through the stacks
like a Cirque du Soleil acrobat.

Straight out of *Jaws* and *Finding Nemo*,
you make me long for Sea World,
where dolphins dive,
male seahorses give birth and
sharks feed on my fantasies.

You flutter through pop culture,
Ice-T, Ice Cube, Jay Z, Beyonce
Mariah's midnight mishap
Kate Hudson's New Year's striptease.

With your scruff beard
and matching mustache
you look properly professorial
even as your hands toss my hair like the pulse of a river.

ANCIENT IMAGES

April when pinks peak,
preening from every tree,
lilacs hint of memory,
the music of sensuality,
and point to days to be.

When your lips
light up my face—
nuzzle my neck—
moments that
make old age ache like puberty.

I dwell on your words
read them like the Koran,
journey with your body language
to temples and stone altars,
cross the Tigris and Euphrates
to ancient days.
Come with me?

ENDINGS

There was a time
of mess kits and pocket knives
charred campfires
back lit ghost tales
and songs of change
damp rec hall dances
choking hairspray odors
early clutching
hidden interracial dating
as we overcame,
but the years passed,
and freedom was overtaken by sprinklers
in the 'burbs.
Upwardly mobile
we forgot overcoming in favor of consumption
and fought for better schools
sent our children to college
our grandchildren to camp
as one by one the past and past lovers passed on.

ABOUT THE AUTHOR

The poetry of Lynn Cohen has been published in many an-
thologies. She was nominated for the 2006 and 2010 Pushcart
Prize for Poetry and has spoken widely on Anglo-Irish Literature
and Modernism and Postmodernism. At Syracuse University,
she was a student and mentee of Pulitzer Prize Winning poets
Stephen Dunn and W. D. Snodgrass. She co-edited *The North
Sea Poetry Scene's LI Sounds III* and *IV* poetry anthologies and
other poetry anthologies. Lynn Cohen teaches at Suffolk County
Community College.

PUBLICATIONS

Dreams and Dreamers (poetry). San Francisco: Blue Light, 2010.

Editor with Tammy Nuzzo-Morgan, Peter Thabit Jones, Edmund Miller, and J. R. Turek. *Long Island Sounds IV.* Southampton: Wild Island, 2009.

Editor with Tammy Nuzzo-Morgan, George Wallace, David B. Axelrod, and J. R. Turek. *Long Island Sounds III.* Southampton: Wild Island, 2008.

Lone Star Days (poetry chapbook). Needmore, PA: Camel, 2004.

With Samuel Cohen. *Tricky Spelling Checker.* International Software, 1985.

"Wrestling with Temptation in George Herbert and Anne Bradstreet." *Cross-Bias No. 12.*

LECTURES

"Intertextuality in Yeats' The Gyres and A Vision." IASIL in Lille, France, July 2014.

"Gerard Manley Hopkins: The Forefront of Modernism." Gerard Manley Hopkins Festival in Ireland, July 2011.

"The Kingfisher as a Recurrent Symbol for Hopkins and Later Poets." Gerard Manley Hopkins Festival in Ireland, July 2009 and published in the Festival's archives.

Irish Studies lecture at Hofstra University. Spring 2011.

T. S. Eliot lecture. National MLA Conference. 1987.

Additional lectures on T. S. Eliot, Dickinson, Fitzgerald, Borges, Sexton, Trethewey, and Coetzee at various venues—including at Hofstra University.

Has given poetry readings in the United States (several at Hofstra) and in Ireland.

GRANTS

As a result of a grant proposal she wrote, the New York State Council for the Humanities awarded the North Sea Poetry Scene a mini-grant for its "Let's Talk Poetry 2008" series. In 2013, as Project Director of Performance Poets Association, she wrote and was awarded a grant by Poets and Writers to feature San Francisco poet Diane Frank on Long Island.

www.ingramcontent.com/pod-product-compliance
Lightning Source LLC
Chambersburg PA
CBHW032027090426
42741CB00006B/755